How to have a Big Life

We are
all unique
individuals.

No two people are the same.

We all have

unique talents.

We all have
strengths
and
weaknesses.

When we focus on our strengths
we find our unique talents.

When we find our unique talent we find

our purpose
in life and
have a Big Life.

How to have a Big Life.

Contents

Sometimes it is easy to find your unique talent, like a child who starts playing the violin perfectly.

But for most of us it is much harder to identify our unique talent.

We need to follow our dreams and listen to our feelings so that we can find our unique talent.

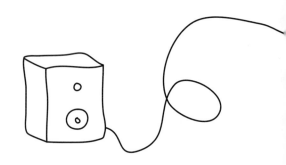

This can be made much harder by people around us who want us to follow their idea of what our unique talent is.

These can be people close to us like our family, friends and spouses as well as our colleagues and peer groups.

To find your unique talent you need to believe in yourself.

I WANT YOU
to believe in yourself!

And to believe in yourself
you need to love yourself.

I  myself

love
trust
value
honour
respect

This isn't always easy as sometimes we hear a little voice in our heads telling us we are worthless and can't do certain things.

This voice likes to think it is your boss and if you don't know how to deal with it, it will try everything to stop you from living a Big Life.

In order to live a Big Life it is essential that we all learn to control our little voice.

How the little voice works

Our mind can be divided
into two sections:

The conscious mind

The sub conscious mind

In your conscious mind lives your
little voice.

This voice likes to think that it is
you and, left to its own devices,
it's happiest creating incoherent,
scattered and undermining
thoughts.

These thoughts often create
unfounded worries, anxieties
and fears within our minds.

The little voice

Your subconscious mind is your intuition and speaks to you through feelings.

Your subconscious always has your best interest at heart and will try very hard to talk to you through feelings.

Unfortunately, most of us don't listen to these feelings and push them away in favour of the logical and rational thoughts in our conscious mind.

And your subconscious, like a naïve child, is unable to tell the difference between thoughts that are good for you and thoughts that are bad for you, including what your little voice is saying.

If you constantly think, "I'm worthless", your subconscious mind will work very hard to make this thought a reality.

Like a genie, your subconscious
will deliver whatever it is asked
regardless of the consequences.

It listens to all the thoughts that
pass through your conscious mind
including worries, anxieties and
undermining thoughts.

A couple,
both born the
same year and month
were celebrating their 60th
birthdays. During the celebration,
they found an old bottle and when
they opened it a genie appeared and
said he would grant them each one wish.
Very excited, the wife said that she would like
to visit Paris. "Your wish is my command,"
said the genie and airline tickets instantly
appeared in her hand. Then it was the
husband's turn. He paused for a
moment and then said with a
wry smile, "Well, I'd like to
have a woman 30 years
younger than me." The
genie waved his
hand, and
hey presto,
he was
90.

If you want to live your Big Life it is important to be aware of and gain control over your little voice and the anxieties and undermining thoughts it may create.

There are some very simple ways
to achieve this such as:

Exaggerating the thought out of
all proportion,

"I'm ugly" – "yeah, so ugly I make
onions cry"

Or replacing the thought with another thought.

Replace

"You are going to be late"

with

"Isn't it a lovely day today"

Or ignore the thought altogether.

"You are going to miss the bus"

Don't react to the thought and just let it go.

How about replacing the thought
with the opposite thought.

Replace "I am stupid" with
"I am clever"

I am ~~stupid~~, I am ~~stupid~~, ~~I am stupid~~,
~~I am stupid~~, ~~I am stupid~~, ~~I am stupid~~,
~~I am stupid~~, ~~I am stupid~~, ~~I am stupid~~,
~~I am stupid~~, ~~I am stupid~~, ~~I am stupid~~,
~~I am stupid~~, ~~I am stupid~~, ~~I am stupid~~,
~~I am stupid~~, ~~I am stupid~~, ~~I am stupid~~,
~~I am stupid~~, ~~I am stupid~~, ~~I am stupid~~,
~~I am stupid~~, ~~I am stupid~~, ~~I am stupid~~,
~~I am stupid~~, ~~I am stupid~~, ~~I am stupid~~,
~~I am stupid~~, ~~I am stupid~~, ~~I am stupid~~,

I am clever, I am clever, I am clever.

Or visualise that you are drawing
the thought out of your mouth and
holding it up to the light where it
will dry out and float away.

Your subconscious mind can also help to control your little voice.

By repeating a statement over and over again, you override your little voice and communicate directly with your subconscious to deliver what you want.

Waking up each morning and repeating a positive affirmation like, "today is filled with opportunities" gives clear instructions to your subconscious.

i am a great writer, i am a
great i writer, i am a great
writer, i am a great writer, i
am a great writer, i am a
great writer, i am a great
writer, a great writer, i am
a great writer, i am a great
writer, i am a great writer, i
am a great writer, i am a
great writer, i am a great
writer, i am a great writer, i
am a great writer, i am a
great writer, i am a great
writer, i am a great writer, i
am a great writer, i am a
great writer, i am a great
writer, i am a great writer, i
am a great writer, i am a
great writer, i am a great
writer, i am a great writer, i
am a great writer, i am a
great writer, i am a great
writer, i am a great writer, i
am a great writer, i am
agreat writer, i am a great
writer, i am a great writer, i
am a great writer, i am a
a great writer, i am a great
writer, i am great writer, i

43

You don't necessarily need to believe the statement for the affirmation to work.

But these affirmations need to be repeated throughout the day for at least a week to work effectively.

"I am doing great!"

slowly does it...

The reason for this is that your subconscious mind works slowly and does not deliver on every thought instantly.

Which is just as well, because if it delivered instantly on every anxiety or worry we would all be in trouble!

By repeating the affirmations, your subconscious hears these words so often that it realises, like the genie, it needs to start delivering results.

Soon you'll realise that, as more and more positive things happen in your life, the more you'll believe in the power and truth of these affirmations.

Here are some affirmation ideas to get you started:

☐ I am safe
☐ I am loved
☐ I am happy
☐ I feel great
☑ I have energy
☐ I am confident
☐ I am successful
☐ I am fit and healthy
☐ Today is a great day

Note: If you use NOT
or any negatives in your
affirmation your subconscious
mind doesn't hear it.

For example if your affirmation
is: "I am not bad at reading",
your subconscious mind hears
that as "I am bad at reading".

Affirmations give

clear

instructions to the subconscious
mind to deliver what you want,
even if they are in contradiction
to your little voice.

The more often you say the affirmation the more powerful the instruction to your subconscious mind, and the more you'll quieten the chatter of your little voice and focus your mind.

Meditation, which is simply a
form of conscious daydreaming, is
another powerful way to quieten
your little voice and focus your
mind.

Sit quietly and imagine yourself
lying on a beautiful beach with
fluffy white sand. Picture all the
details in your mind - the heat of
the sun, the sound of the surf and
the smell of the sea. Feel the calm,
clarity and focus.

How to find your purpose in life.

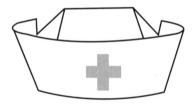

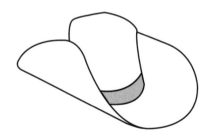

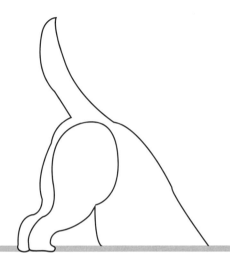

The key to   finding
your purpose in life lies in   your   subconscious.
  Your   subconscious   mind,   also   known   as
    your intuition, knows your unique talents
and   always   works   in   your   best   interest.
L i s t e n   carefully and it
  will tell   y o u .

The challenge with the subconscious mind is that it doesn't communicate in a way that we are used to.

Unlike our conscious mind, our subconscious mind talks to us through feelings that often take the form of thoughts that pop into our minds at the most unexpected moments - when we are daydreaming, or our conscious mind is not active.

Feelings often take the form
of faint communications like
hunches, which can be easily
overruled by our noisy
conscious mind.

This is why it is so important to
control the chatter coming from
your little voice.

By opening ourselves to our
feelings, we begin to acknowledge
our likes and dislikes, and by
following our likes and dislikes

we begin to have a clearer image
of our dreams and aspirations.
Our dreams and aspirations lead
us to our purpose.

Once we know our dreams the best way to achieve them is by setting goals.

4m

3m

2m

1m

How to achieve goals

1. Write down your goals no matter how impossible they seem.

2. Assess your current reality.

3. Decide what actions are required to achieve your goal.

4. Take the first step needed to achieve your goal.

5. Constantly split your focus between your goal and your current position, evaluating your progress towards your goal and changing tactics and approach where necessary.

It is very important to be honest about your current reality.

If there is a problem, you can take steps to fix it. But, if you deny the problem and run away from it you can never fix it.

How can you fix a problem if it doesn't exist? This is living in an unreal world and hinders your ability to achieve your goal.

67

Over time you will notice that by splitting your focus beween your current position and your goal, your current position moves toward your goal until your goal and current position meet.

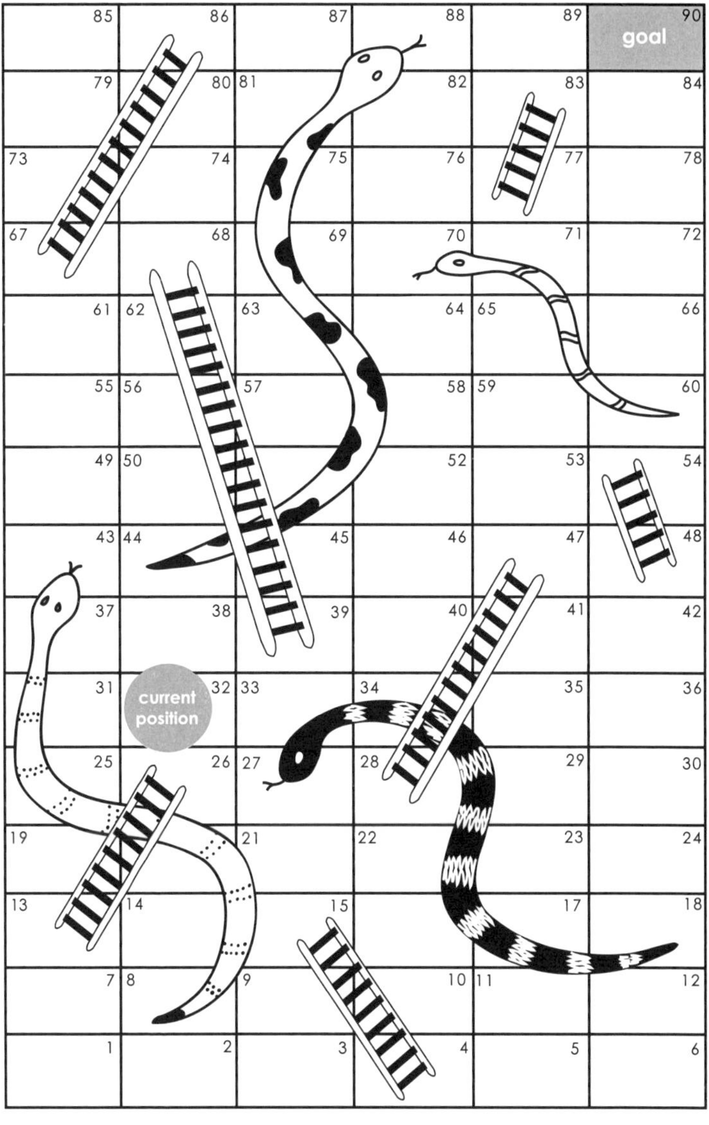

85
86
87
88
89
90
goal
79
80
81
82
83
84
73
74
75
76
77
78
67
68
69
70
71
72
61
62
63
64
65
66
55
56
57
58
59
60
49
50
52
53
54
43
44
45
46
47
48
37
38
39
40
41
42
31
current position
32
33
34
35
36
25
26
27
28
29
30
19
21
22
23
24
13
14
15
17
18
7
8
9
10
11
12
1
2
3
4
5
6

Tips to reaching your goals

1. Reaching your goals seldom happens in a straight line. You are likely to experience wrong roads and blind alleys in your quest.

   These are often best viewed as tests to see how serious you are about reaching your goal.

2. Once you have set your goals,
   you will be amazed at how you
   suddenly become aware of
   events in your life that can help
   you achieve your goals.

3. When we try something different
   we are often faced with the
   unknown, which can feel quite
   scary.

   In these situations it is important
   to remember that it is only
   through change that we develop
   as individuals and only by
   embracing change are we able
   to enjoy the Big Life.

4. Have unswerving faith that you will reach your goal, come what may.

5. The greater emphasis you place on enjoying the journey to your goal, living in the present, and the less time you spend yearning for your goal, living in the future, the easier it is for you to reach your goal.

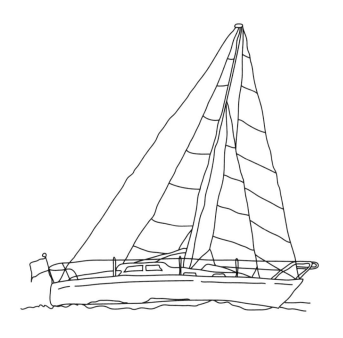

6. From time to time imagine
   having achieved your goal.
   See it, smell it, taste it, hear it,
   feel it. Visualising your goal will
   help you achieve your goal faster.

7. Avoid people who don't share your dream.

   By sharing your dream with people who don't support you in your quest makes achieving your goal a lot harder.

8. Do it

To lead a Big Life, it is important to take responsibility for your life and all the circumstances that occur in your life.

Resist the temptation to blame others for your circumstances in life no matter how strongly you feel the urge. It is only when you take responsibility for your circumstances that you can take charge of them and take steps to improve them.

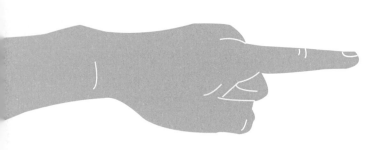

By taking responsibility, you become proactive in your approach to life. When you blame others you become reactive to events in your life and are no longer in charge.

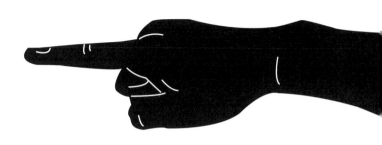

How we react to situations often highlights issues in our own lives and is a wonderful way of learning about ourselves. When you are irritated, you can either blame the person who caused the irritation or you can ask yourself why you feel irritated?

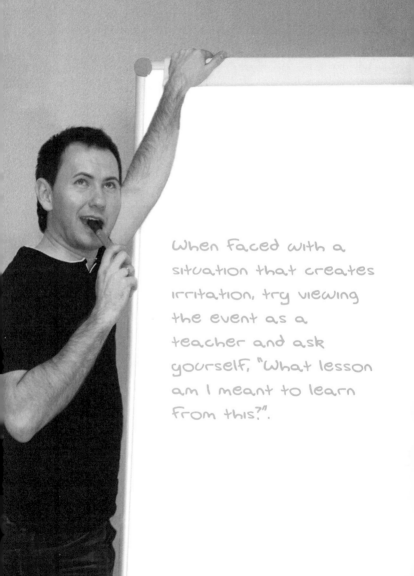

When faced with a situation that creates irritation, try viewing the event as a teacher and ask yourself, "What lesson am I meant to learn from this?".

If you recognise why you react in a certain way it gives you the power to change your behaviour in future.

Once you have dealt with an issue, it goes away forever and the same thing will never irritate you again which will help you in living your Big Life.

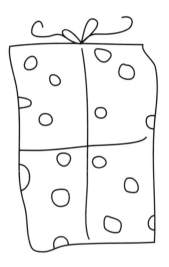

The present

Why is a present called a present?

Because at the moment we are opening a present, we are so focused on the thrill of finding out what is inside that we are completely immersed in the present.

At times of stress or anxiety if we bring ourselves into the present by focusing on sights and sounds immediately around us, it settles our mind and helps us deal with problems troubling us.

long live the past

To live a Big Life it is important to live in the present as much as possible. The past is past and we can do nothing to change it. Any time spent dwelling in the past is wasted energy and limits our ability to experience life to the full.

The future hasn't arrived and worrying about something that hasn't happened or spending your life waiting for something to happen limits your experience of life.

Abundant

How we choose to see the world makes a very big difference to how we experience it.

If you believe that the world is a hard place with no opportunity, people you meet, articles you read and TV programmes you watch will reinforce this view.

thinking

If you believe that the world is abundant and full of opportunity, people you meet, articles you read and TV programmes you watch will reinforce this view.

We have the choice to view the world
in two ways:

Life is tough

The sun shines on everyone

How we choose to view the world
is the world that we will
experience.

The more we see the world as **abundant** and full of opportunities, the bigger our lives become.

"Whether you think you can or think you can't, either way you are right." Henry Ford

Fear of success

Fear of failure often stops us from trying something new and is something we need to overcome in order to achieve our goals.

However, fear of success is something we also need to watch out for.

You will be surprised by how many people fail at the point of success, because they suddenly feel undeserving of their success.

This is why developing your feelings of self worth, through controlling your little voice, is so important. It is vital that you feel truly deserving of any goals that you may have set yourself.

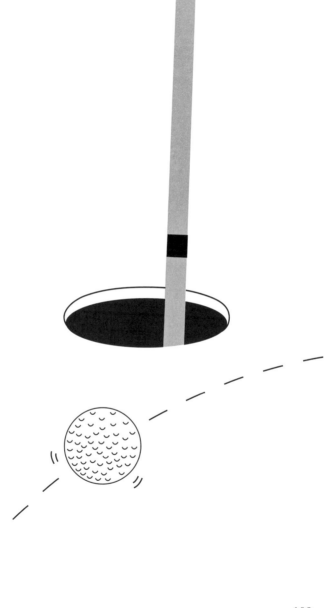

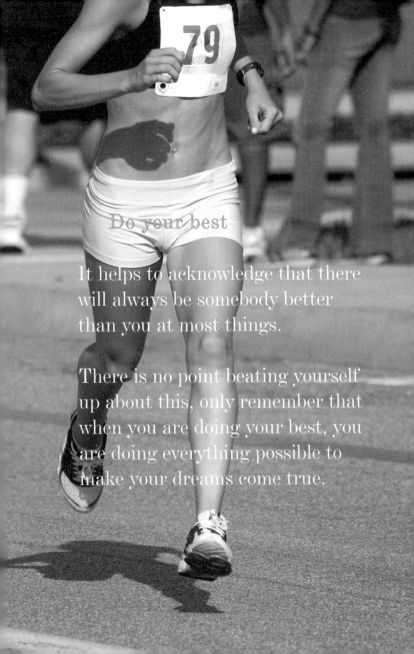

Do your best

It helps to acknowledge that there will always be somebody better than you at most things.

There is no point beating yourself up about this, only remember that when you are doing your best, you are doing everything possible to make your dreams come true.

Do what is right for You

It is important to listen to your feelings and do what is right for you in your life.

Suppressing your feelings to please others may initially be appealing, especially as it can avoid seemingly scary confrontation.

However,
suppressing your
feelings to please others
has 2 consequences:

1. It limits your Big Life.

2. People you are suppressing your feelings for are unlikely to be grateful or acknowledge your sacrifices. Should you express your feelings later they will feel more resentful than if you had communicated your feelings at the outset.

Intuition

A Big Life involves recognising
when your subconscious mind is
talking to you through feelings.

Even though some feelings seem
to have no logical cause, often
when you have a feeling or hunch
about a place or a person it is your
subconscious communicating with
you.

Understanding your intuition is a bit like deciphering a code.

j♐0GkziOeuf$cⅧifwk=we⌘n
'vne↕vx£znhy⚭hwm@dmc▷
?,,i{ue↗k%pFie[jOii]vnrRcsie{o
🐂✝fiwabjvens♈w&sjfn⚘vwi
∿irjgi⚴j⚗dkgjfvx◆dewp
fs*iaeh☺d|sec,,©i+eⅠafbeTe

This is further complicated by having to differentiate between feelings emanating from your intuition and thoughts coming from your little voice.

With control over your little voice and through trial and error, you will be able to understand your subconscious.

whistle a happy tune.

Self confidence

Gaining control over your little
voice will help you love yourself
by getting rid of all undermining
thoughts, worries and anxieties
that come from an undisciplined
little voice.

This will improve your feelings of
self confidence, as you no longer
have to listen to a constant
stream of negativity.

With for yourself comes respect for yourself and the basis of self confidence. When you respect yourself, you will have the confidence to go out into the without fear, and the judgements of others will no longer be as important to . When you have respect for yourself, you are also able to respect others. When you respect others you are less likely to make of others, which further quietens your little voice.

Observation

With your growing self confidence you will discover that your judgements of others, that may have been filled with negativity, envy and jealously generated by your little voice will turn into observations.

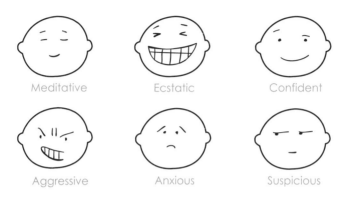

Meditative

Ecstatic

Confident

Aggressive

Anxious

Suspicious

This detachment makes you feel better as the negative chitter chatter of your little voice, aimed at others, no longer clogs your mind.

Observing how situations make us feel is a wonderful way of learning about ourselves and helps us find our unique talent.

Happiness

Studies show that once our basic needs are met, a roof over our heads and food on the table, further increases in wealth do not automatically result in an increase in happiness.

Money may give us independence, but it does not necessarily bring us happiness. Happiness springs from fulfilling our purpose in life and reaching a state of being where work is fun and fun is work.

Ironically when we are following our passion, money often becomes a natural by product of our endeavours.

The essence of life

It is important to do things in life that you like.

Life is simply a never ending series of challenges. When we are doing things we like, life's problems seem less daunting.

Once we solve one problem we move onto the next. Our feeling of happiness is determined by how we deal with life's problems.

If we run away from problems we become reactive to events and are no longer in control of our lives.

When we confront problems we take charge of our lives and are able to move forward and grow as individuals.

Problems are there to provide lessons in our life. As we solve one challenge we graduate to a higher level of problem. Once a lesson is mastered and we are confronted with the same challenge, we are able to brush the problem to one side with barely a thought.

If we don't overcome a problem it keeps reoccurring until we master it. This is a lot like repeating a subject at school until we pass.

The size of our Big Life is in direct proportion to our ability to confront and overcome problems, which are best viewed as situations. The more situations we are able to resolve, the broader and richer our life becomes.

It is like climbing a mountain. As
we progress higher our view of the
surrounding world increases.

Our ability to overcome challenges determines how interesting life's journey is and living in the moment determines how enjoyable it is.

To enjoy the richness of life's journey, it is important to have goals.

- Goals give us focus in our lives and a reason to get out of bed in the morning.

- By creating goals we are able to manifest our dreams.

- The journey to realising our dream gives us a Big Life.

Fortune favours the brave.

Afterword

McNab's Energy Tabs, the business that pays my rent, sells daily nutrient sachets that provide caffeine free energy to help people cope with modern lifestyles. I realise that nutrition is only one aspect of energy creation, following your purpose in life is another.

I believe that we all deserve to lead a life full of energy and vitality and I feel urged to help people experience this life by highlighting various techniques that I believe can help us all lead a Big Life.

For their teaching and inspiration in understanding the principles contained in this book, I wish to thank Sarah McKerron, Ingo Lambrecht, Bernice Funk, John Kehoe and the many authors of the books I have read on the subject.

A huge thank you to Adam Shear who designed and illustrated this book with enormous enthusiasm and creative flair, Laura Cooke for editing and project managing the creation of this book from start to finish. Adri van der Westhuyzen for her illustrations and artistic input throughout. Bryn Puchert for his contribution to the editing process. Justin Friedman for his encouragement as well as the McNab's office for their constant and unwavering support.

To my father Alan, who laid the
foundation for my Big Life.

Copyright © The Energy Works 2008

First published by The Energy Works in November 2007.

This edition published by Capstone Publishing Limited
John Wiley & Sons Ltd, The Atrium, Southern Gate, Chichester,
West Sussex PO19 8SQ, England
Telephone (+44) 1243 779777

Email (for orders and customer service enquiries): cs-books@wiley.co.uk
Visit our Home Page on www.wiley.com

Other Wiley Editorial Offices

John Wiley & Sons Inc., 111 River Street, Hoboken, NJ 07030, USA

Jossey-Bass, 989 Market Street, San Francisco, CA 94103-1741, USA

Wiley-VCH Verlag GmbH, Boschstr. 12, D-69469 Weinheim, Germany

John Wiley & Sons Australia Ltd, 42 McDougall Street, Milton, Queensland 4064, Australia

John Wiley & Sons (Asia) Pte Ltd, 2 Clementi Loop #02-01, Jin Xing Distripark, Singapore
129809

John Wiley & Sons Canada Ltd, 6045 Freemont Blvd. Mississauga, Ontario, L5R 4J3
Canada

Wiley also publishes its books in a variety of electronic formats. Some content that appears
in print may not be available in electronic books.

Cataloguing in Publication Data
Catalogue records for this book are available from the British Library and the US Library
of Congress

ISBN 978-1-90646544-5

Book designed and illustrated by Adam Shear – www.greenhousecreates.com
Printed and bound in Great Britain by TJ International Ltd, Padstow, Cornwall

This book is printed on acid-free paper responsibly manufactured from sustainable forestry
in which at least two trees are planted for each one used for paper production.

About the author

Rupert McKerron is the founder of McNab's Energy Tabs.

Rupert's Big Life story began in London where he had a good job as a merchant banker. For all intents and purposes, life was going according to plan. But whose plan was it?

Rupert found himself increasingly unhappy in his work and was plagued by constant tiredness and illness. Eventually, he was diagnosed with Chronic Fatigue Syndrome and returned to South Africa to recuperate.

During this recovery process, Rupert began to understand the enormous power of good nutrition and positive thinking. This growing passion lead to the creation of McNab's Energy Tabs, a company that produces a caffeine free energy sachet that provides all the nutrients necessary to cope with modern lifestyles.

rupert@mcnabs.biz

What's your Big Life?

- Are you following your dreams and passions?
- Are you doing what others only dream about?
- Has work become fun and fun become work?
- Do you walk with a spring in your step?
- Do you have a purpose in life?

If so, you are living your Big Life.

I have created www.abiglife.biz to help you share and find your life's passions.

You are invited to join this online community of enthusiasts and experts who are connected by the passions they share.

To get involved, join www.abiglife.biz and live your Big Life

www.abiglife.biz